Guest List Planner

Name
Address
Telephone Number
E-mail Address
Gift

Save The Day Card Sent	Invitation Sent	R.S.V.P Received	Thank You Sent	Number Attending

Name
Address
Telephone Number
E-mail Address
Gift

Save The Day Card Sent	Invitation Sent	R.S.V.P Received	Thank You Sent	Number Attending

Name
Address
Telephone Number
E-mail Address
Gift

Save The Day Card Sent	Invitation Sent	R.S.V.P Received	Thank You Sent	Number Attending

Name
Address
Telephone Number
E-mail Address
Gift

Save The Day Card Sent	Invitation Sent	R.S.V.P Received	Thank You Sent	Number Attending

Name
Address
Telephone Number
E-mail Address
Gift

Save The Day Card Sent	Invitation Sent	R.S.V.P Received	Thank You Sent	Number Attending

Guest List Planner

Name

Address

Telephone Number

E-mail Address

Gift

Save The Day Card Sent	Invitation Sent	R.S.V.P Received	Thank You Sent	Number Attending

Name

Address

Telephone Number

E-mail Address

Gift

Save The Day Card Sent	Invitation Sent	R.S.V.P Received	Thank You Sent	Number Attending

Name

Address

Telephone Number

E-mail Address

Gift

Save The Day Card Sent	Invitation Sent	R.S.V.P Received	Thank You Sent	Number Attending

Name

Address

Telephone Number

E-mail Address

Gift

Save The Day Card Sent	Invitation Sent	R.S.V.P Received	Thank You Sent	Number Attending

Name

Address

Telephone Number

E-mail Address

Gift

Save The Day Card Sent	Invitation Sent	R.S.V.P Received	Thank You Sent	Number Attending

Guest List Planner

Name

Address

Telephone Number

E-mail Address

Gift

Save The Day Card Sent	Invitation Sent	R.S.V.P Received	Thank You Sent	Number Attending

Name

Address

Telephone Number

E-mail Address

Gift

Save The Day Card Sent	Invitation Sent	R.S.V.P Received	Thank You Sent	Number Attending

Name

Address

Telephone Number

E-mail Address

Gift

Save The Day Card Sent	Invitation Sent	R.S.V.P Received	Thank You Sent	Number Attending

Name

Address

Telephone Number

E-mail Address

Gift

Save The Day Card Sent	Invitation Sent	R.S.V.P Received	Thank You Sent	Number Attending

Name

Address

Telephone Number

E-mail Address

Gift

Save The Day Card Sent	Invitation Sent	R.S.V.P Received	Thank You Sent	Number Attending

Guest List Planner

Name
Address
Telephone Number
E-mail Address
Gift

| Save The Day Card Sent | Invitation Sent | R.S.V.P Received | Thank You Sent | Number Attending |

Name
Address
Telephone Number
E-mail Address
Gift

| Save The Day Card Sent | Invitation Sent | R.S.V.P Received | Thank You Sent | Number Attending |

Name
Address
Telephone Number
E-mail Address
Gift

| Save The Day Card Sent | Invitation Sent | R.S.V.P Received | Thank You Sent | Number Attending |

Name
Address
Telephone Number
E-mail Address
Gift

| Save The Day Card Sent | Invitation Sent | R.S.V.P Received | Thank You Sent | Number Attending |

Name
Address
Telephone Number
E-mail Address
Gift

| Save The Day Card Sent | Invitation Sent | R.S.V.P Received | Thank You Sent | Number Attending |

Guest List Planner

Name

Address

Telephone Number

E-mail Address

Gift

| Save The Day Card Sent | Invitation Sent | R.S.V.P Received | Thank You Sent | Number Attending |

Name

Address

Telephone Number

E-mail Address

Gift

| Save The Day Card Sent | Invitation Sent | R.S.V.P Received | Thank You Sent | Number Attending |

Name

Address

Telephone Number

E-mail Address

Gift

| Save The Day Card Sent | Invitation Sent | R.S.V.P Received | Thank You Sent | Number Attending |

Name

Address

Telephone Number

E-mail Address

Gift

| Save The Day Card Sent | Invitation Sent | R.S.V.P Received | Thank You Sent | Number Attending |

Name

Address

Telephone Number

E-mail Address

Gift

| Save The Day Card Sent | Invitation Sent | R.S.V.P Received | Thank You Sent | Number Attending |

Guest List Planner

Name

Address

Telephone Number

E-mail Address

Gift

Save The Day Card Sent	Invitation Sent	R.S.V.P Received	Thank You Sent	Number Attending

Name

Address

Telephone Number

E-mail Address

Gift

Save The Day Card Sent	Invitation Sent	R.S.V.P Received	Thank You Sent	Number Attending

Name

Address

Telephone Number

E-mail Address

Gift

Save The Day Card Sent	Invitation Sent	R.S.V.P Received	Thank You Sent	Number Attending

Name

Address

Telephone Number

E-mail Address

Gift

Save The Day Card Sent	Invitation Sent	R.S.V.P Received	Thank You Sent	Number Attending

Name

Address

Telephone Number

E-mail Address

Gift

Save The Day Card Sent	Invitation Sent	R.S.V.P Received	Thank You Sent	Number Attending

Guest List Planner

Name

Address

Telephone Number

E-mail Address

Gift

Save The Day Card Sent	Invitation Sent	R.S.V.P Received	Thank You Sent	Number Attending

Name

Address

Telephone Number

E-mail Address

Gift

Save The Day Card Sent	Invitation Sent	R.S.V.P Received	Thank You Sent	Number Attending

Name

Address

Telephone Number

E-mail Address

Gift

Save The Day Card Sent	Invitation Sent	R.S.V.P Received	Thank You Sent	Number Attending

Name

Address

Telephone Number

E-mail Address

Gift

Save The Day Card Sent	Invitation Sent	R.S.V.P Received	Thank You Sent	Number Attending

Name

Address

Telephone Number

E-mail Address

Gift

Save The Day Card Sent	Invitation Sent	R.S.V.P Received	Thank You Sent	Number Attending

Guest List Planner

Name

Address

Telephone Number

E-mail Address

Gift

Save The Day Card Sent	Invitation Sent	R.S.V.P Received	Thank You Sent	Number Attending

Name

Address

Telephone Number

E-mail Address

Gift

Save The Day Card Sent	Invitation Sent	R.S.V.P Received	Thank You Sent	Number Attending

Name

Address

Telephone Number

E-mail Address

Gift

Save The Day Card Sent	Invitation Sent	R.S.V.P Received	Thank You Sent	Number Attending

Name

Address

Telephone Number

E-mail Address

Gift

Save The Day Card Sent	Invitation Sent	R.S.V.P Received	Thank You Sent	Number Attending

Name

Address

Telephone Number

E-mail Address

Gift

Save The Day Card Sent	Invitation Sent	R.S.V.P Received	Thank You Sent	Number Attending

Guest List Planner

Name

Address

Telephone Number

E-mail Address

Gift

| Save The Day Card Sent | Invitation Sent | R.S.V.P Received | Thank You Sent | Number Attending |

Name

Address

Telephone Number

E-mail Address

Gift

| Save The Day Card Sent | Invitation Sent | R.S.V.P Received | Thank You Sent | Number Attending |

Name

Address

Telephone Number

E-mail Address

Gift

| Save The Day Card Sent | Invitation Sent | R.S.V.P Received | Thank You Sent | Number Attending |

Name

Address

Telephone Number

E-mail Address

Gift

| Save The Day Card Sent | Invitation Sent | R.S.V.P Received | Thank You Sent | Number Attending |

Name

Address

Telephone Number

E-mail Address

Gift

| Save The Day Card Sent | Invitation Sent | R.S.V.P Received | Thank You Sent | Number Attending |

Guest List Planner

Name
Address
Telephone Number
E-mail Address
Gift

Save The Day Card Sent	Invitation Sent	R.S.V.P Received	Thank You Sent	Number Attending

Name
Address
Telephone Number
E-mail Address
Gift

Save The Day Card Sent	Invitation Sent	R.S.V.P Received	Thank You Sent	Number Attending

Name
Address
Telephone Number
E-mail Address
Gift

Save The Day Card Sent	Invitation Sent	R.S.V.P Received	Thank You Sent	Number Attending

Name
Address
Telephone Number
E-mail Address
Gift

Save The Day Card Sent	Invitation Sent	R.S.V.P Received	Thank You Sent	Number Attending

Name
Address
Telephone Number
E-mail Address
Gift

Save The Day Card Sent	Invitation Sent	R.S.V.P Received	Thank You Sent	Number Attending

Guest List Planner

Name
Address
Telephone Number
E-mail Address
Gift

Save The Day Card Sent	Invitation Sent	R.S.V.P Received	Thank You Sent	Number Attending

Name
Address
Telephone Number
E-mail Address
Gift

Save The Day Card Sent	Invitation Sent	R.S.V.P Received	Thank You Sent	Number Attending

Name
Address
Telephone Number
E-mail Address
Gift

Save The Day Card Sent	Invitation Sent	R.S.V.P Received	Thank You Sent	Number Attending

Name
Address
Telephone Number
E-mail Address
Gift

Save The Day Card Sent	Invitation Sent	R.S.V.P Received	Thank You Sent	Number Attending

Name
Address
Telephone Number
E-mail Address
Gift

Save The Day Card Sent	Invitation Sent	R.S.V.P Received	Thank You Sent	Number Attending

Guest List Planner

Name

Address

Telephone Number

E-mail Address

Gift

Save The Day Card Sent	Invitation Sent	R.S.V.P Received	Thank You Sent	Number Attending

Name

Address

Telephone Number

E-mail Address

Gift

Save The Day Card Sent	Invitation Sent	R.S.V.P Received	Thank You Sent	Number Attending

Name

Address

Telephone Number

E-mail Address

Gift

Save The Day Card Sent	Invitation Sent	R.S.V.P Received	Thank You Sent	Number Attending

Name

Address

Telephone Number

E-mail Address

Gift

Save The Day Card Sent	Invitation Sent	R.S.V.P Received	Thank You Sent	Number Attending

Name

Address

Telephone Number

E-mail Address

Gift

Save The Day Card Sent	Invitation Sent	R.S.V.P Received	Thank You Sent	Number Attending

Guest List Planner

Name

Address

Telephone Number

E-mail Address

Gift

Save The Day Card Sent	Invitation Sent	R.S.V.P Received	Thank You Sent	Number Attending

Name

Address

Telephone Number

E-mail Address

Gift

Save The Day Card Sent	Invitation Sent	R.S.V.P Received	Thank You Sent	Number Attending

Name

Address

Telephone Number

E-mail Address

Gift

Save The Day Card Sent	Invitation Sent	R.S.V.P Received	Thank You Sent	Number Attending

Name

Address

Telephone Number

E-mail Address

Gift

Save The Day Card Sent	Invitation Sent	R.S.V.P Received	Thank You Sent	Number Attending

Name

Address

Telephone Number

E-mail Address

Gift

Save The Day Card Sent	Invitation Sent	R.S.V.P Received	Thank You Sent	Number Attending

Guest List Planner

Name
_____

Address
_____

Telephone Number
_____

E-mail Address
_____

Gift
_____

Save The Day Card Sent	Invitation Sent	R.S.V.P Received	Thank You Sent	Number Attending
_____	_____	_____	_____	_____

Name
_____

Address
_____

Telephone Number
_____

E-mail Address
_____

Gift
_____

Save The Day Card Sent	Invitation Sent	R.S.V.P Received	Thank You Sent	Number Attending
_____	_____	_____	_____	_____

Name
_____

Address
_____

Telephone Number
_____

E-mail Address
_____

Gift
_____

Save The Day Card Sent	Invitation Sent	R.S.V.P Received	Thank You Sent	Number Attending
_____	_____	_____	_____	_____

Name
_____

Address
_____

Telephone Number
_____

E-mail Address
_____

Gift
_____

Save The Day Card Sent	Invitation Sent	R.S.V.P Received	Thank You Sent	Number Attending
_____	_____	_____	_____	_____

Name
_____

Address
_____

Telephone Number
_____

E-mail Address
_____

Gift
_____

Save The Day Card Sent	Invitation Sent	R.S.V.P Received	Thank You Sent	Number Attending
_____	_____	_____	_____	_____

Guest List Planner

Name

Address

Telephone Number

E-mail Address

Gift

Save The Day Card Sent	Invitation Sent	R.S.V.P Received	Thank You Sent	Number Attending

Name

Address

Telephone Number

E-mail Address

Gift

Save The Day Card Sent	Invitation Sent	R.S.V.P Received	Thank You Sent	Number Attending

Name

Address

Telephone Number

E-mail Address

Gift

Save The Day Card Sent	Invitation Sent	R.S.V.P Received	Thank You Sent	Number Attending

Name

Address

Telephone Number

E-mail Address

Gift

Save The Day Card Sent	Invitation Sent	R.S.V.P Received	Thank You Sent	Number Attending

Name

Address

Telephone Number

E-mail Address

Gift

Save The Day Card Sent	Invitation Sent	R.S.V.P Received	Thank You Sent	Number Attending

Guest List Planner

Name

Address

Telephone Number

E-mail Address

Gift

Save The Day Card Sent	Invitation Sent	R.S.V.P Received	Thank You Sent	Number Attending

Name

Address

Telephone Number

E-mail Address

Gift

Save The Day Card Sent	Invitation Sent	R.S.V.P Received	Thank You Sent	Number Attending

Name

Address

Telephone Number

E-mail Address

Gift

Save The Day Card Sent	Invitation Sent	R.S.V.P Received	Thank You Sent	Number Attending

Name

Address

Telephone Number

E-mail Address

Gift

Save The Day Card Sent	Invitation Sent	R.S.V.P Received	Thank You Sent	Number Attending

Name

Address

Telephone Number

E-mail Address

Gift

Save The Day Card Sent	Invitation Sent	R.S.V.P Received	Thank You Sent	Number Attending

Guest List Planner

Name _____
Address _____
Telephone Number _____
E-mail Address _____
Gift _____

Save The Day Card Sent	Invitation Sent	R.S.V.P Received	Thank You Sent	Number Attending

Name _____
Address _____
Telephone Number _____
E-mail Address _____
Gift _____

Save The Day Card Sent	Invitation Sent	R.S.V.P Received	Thank You Sent	Number Attending

Name _____
Address _____
Telephone Number _____
E-mail Address _____
Gift _____

Save The Day Card Sent	Invitation Sent	R.S.V.P Received	Thank You Sent	Number Attending

Name _____
Address _____
Telephone Number _____
E-mail Address _____
Gift _____

Save The Day Card Sent	Invitation Sent	R.S.V.P Received	Thank You Sent	Number Attending

Name _____
Address _____
Telephone Number _____
E-mail Address _____
Gift _____

Save The Day Card Sent	Invitation Sent	R.S.V.P Received	Thank You Sent	Number Attending

Guest List Planner

Name

Address

Telephone Number

E-mail Address

Gift

| Save The Day Card Sent | Invitation Sent | R.S.V.P Received | Thank You Sent | Number Attending |

Name

Address

Telephone Number

E-mail Address

Gift

| Save The Day Card Sent | Invitation Sent | R.S.V.P Received | Thank You Sent | Number Attending |

Name

Address

Telephone Number

E-mail Address

Gift

| Save The Day Card Sent | Invitation Sent | R.S.V.P Received | Thank You Sent | Number Attending |

Name

Address

Telephone Number

E-mail Address

Gift

| Save The Day Card Sent | Invitation Sent | R.S.V.P Received | Thank You Sent | Number Attending |

Name

Address

Telephone Number

E-mail Address

Gift

| Save The Day Card Sent | Invitation Sent | R.S.V.P Received | Thank You Sent | Number Attending |

Guest List Planner

Name _____
Address _____
Telephone Number _____
E-mail Address _____
Gift _____

Save The Day Card Sent	Invitation Sent	R.S.V.P Received	Thank You Sent	Number Attending

Name _____
Address _____
Telephone Number _____
E-mail Address _____
Gift _____

Save The Day Card Sent	Invitation Sent	R.S.V.P Received	Thank You Sent	Number Attending

Name _____
Address _____
Telephone Number _____
E-mail Address _____
Gift _____

Save The Day Card Sent	Invitation Sent	R.S.V.P Received	Thank You Sent	Number Attending

Name _____
Address _____
Telephone Number _____
E-mail Address _____
Gift _____

Save The Day Card Sent	Invitation Sent	R.S.V.P Received	Thank You Sent	Number Attending

Name _____
Address _____
Telephone Number _____
E-mail Address _____
Gift _____

Save The Day Card Sent	Invitation Sent	R.S.V.P Received	Thank You Sent	Number Attending

Guest List Planner

Name

Address

Telephone Number

E-mail Address

Gift

Save The Day Card Sent	Invitation Sent	R.S.V.P Received	Thank You Sent	Number Attending

Name

Address

Telephone Number

E-mail Address

Gift

Save The Day Card Sent	Invitation Sent	R.S.V.P Received	Thank You Sent	Number Attending

Name

Address

Telephone Number

E-mail Address

Gift

Save The Day Card Sent	Invitation Sent	R.S.V.P Received	Thank You Sent	Number Attending

Name

Address

Telephone Number

E-mail Address

Gift

Save The Day Card Sent	Invitation Sent	R.S.V.P Received	Thank You Sent	Number Attending

Name

Address

Telephone Number

E-mail Address

Gift

Save The Day Card Sent	Invitation Sent	R.S.V.P Received	Thank You Sent	Number Attending

Guest List Planner

Name

Address

Telephone Number

E-mail Address

Gift

Save The Day Card Sent	Invitation Sent	R.S.V.P Received	Thank You Sent	Number Attending

Name

Address

Telephone Number

E-mail Address

Gift

Save The Day Card Sent	Invitation Sent	R.S.V.P Received	Thank You Sent	Number Attending

Name

Address

Telephone Number

E-mail Address

Gift

Save The Day Card Sent	Invitation Sent	R.S.V.P Received	Thank You Sent	Number Attending

Name

Address

Telephone Number

E-mail Address

Gift

Save The Day Card Sent	Invitation Sent	R.S.V.P Received	Thank You Sent	Number Attending

Name

Address

Telephone Number

E-mail Address

Gift

Save The Day Card Sent	Invitation Sent	R.S.V.P Received	Thank You Sent	Number Attending

Guest List Planner

Name

Address

Telephone Number

E-mail Address

Gift

Save The Day Card Sent	Invitation Sent	R.S.V.P Received	Thank You Sent	Number Attending

Name

Address

Telephone Number

E-mail Address

Gift

Save The Day Card Sent	Invitation Sent	R.S.V.P Received	Thank You Sent	Number Attending

Name

Address

Telephone Number

E-mail Address

Gift

Save The Day Card Sent	Invitation Sent	R.S.V.P Received	Thank You Sent	Number Attending

Name

Address

Telephone Number

E-mail Address

Gift

Save The Day Card Sent	Invitation Sent	R.S.V.P Received	Thank You Sent	Number Attending

Name

Address

Telephone Number

E-mail Address

Gift

Save The Day Card Sent	Invitation Sent	R.S.V.P Received	Thank You Sent	Number Attending

Guest List Planner

Name

Address

Telephone Number

E-mail Address

Gift

Save The Day Card Sent	Invitation Sent	R.S.V.P Received	Thank You Sent	Number Attending

Name

Address

Telephone Number

E-mail Address

Gift

Save The Day Card Sent	Invitation Sent	R.S.V.P Received	Thank You Sent	Number Attending

Name

Address

Telephone Number

E-mail Address

Gift

Save The Day Card Sent	Invitation Sent	R.S.V.P Received	Thank You Sent	Number Attending

Name

Address

Telephone Number

E-mail Address

Gift

Save The Day Card Sent	Invitation Sent	R.S.V.P Received	Thank You Sent	Number Attending

Name

Address

Telephone Number

E-mail Address

Gift

Save The Day Card Sent	Invitation Sent	R.S.V.P Received	Thank You Sent	Number Attending

Guest List Planner

Name _____

Address _____

Telephone Number _____

E-mail Address _____

Gift _____

Save The Day Card Sent	Invitation Sent	R.S.V.P Received	Thank You Sent	Number Attending
_____	_____	_____	_____	_____

Name _____

Address _____

Telephone Number _____

E-mail Address _____

Gift _____

Save The Day Card Sent	Invitation Sent	R.S.V.P Received	Thank You Sent	Number Attending
_____	_____	_____	_____	_____

Name _____

Address _____

Telephone Number _____

E-mail Address _____

Gift _____

Save The Day Card Sent	Invitation Sent	R.S.V.P Received	Thank You Sent	Number Attending
_____	_____	_____	_____	_____

Name _____

Address _____

Telephone Number _____

E-mail Address _____

Gift _____

Save The Day Card Sent	Invitation Sent	R.S.V.P Received	Thank You Sent	Number Attending
_____	_____	_____	_____	_____

Name _____

Address _____

Telephone Number _____

E-mail Address _____

Gift _____

Save The Day Card Sent	Invitation Sent	R.S.V.P Received	Thank You Sent	Number Attending
_____	_____	_____	_____	_____

Guest List Planner

Name

Address

Telephone Number

E-mail Address

Gift

Save The Day Card Sent	Invitation Sent	R.S.V.P Received	Thank You Sent	Number Attending

Name

Address

Telephone Number

E-mail Address

Gift

Save The Day Card Sent	Invitation Sent	R.S.V.P Received	Thank You Sent	Number Attending

Name

Address

Telephone Number

E-mail Address

Gift

Save The Day Card Sent	Invitation Sent	R.S.V.P Received	Thank You Sent	Number Attending

Name

Address

Telephone Number

E-mail Address

Gift

Save The Day Card Sent	Invitation Sent	R.S.V.P Received	Thank You Sent	Number Attending

Name

Address

Telephone Number

E-mail Address

Gift

Save The Day Card Sent	Invitation Sent	R.S.V.P Received	Thank You Sent	Number Attending

Guest List Planner

Name

Address

Telephone Number

E-mail Address

Gift

Save The Day Card Sent	Invitation Sent	R.S.V.P Received	Thank You Sent	Number Attending

Name

Address

Telephone Number

E-mail Address

Gift

Save The Day Card Sent	Invitation Sent	R.S.V.P Received	Thank You Sent	Number Attending

Name

Address

Telephone Number

E-mail Address

Gift

Save The Day Card Sent	Invitation Sent	R.S.V.P Received	Thank You Sent	Number Attending

Name

Address

Telephone Number

E-mail Address

Gift

Save The Day Card Sent	Invitation Sent	R.S.V.P Received	Thank You Sent	Number Attending

Name

Address

Telephone Number

E-mail Address

Gift

Save The Day Card Sent	Invitation Sent	R.S.V.P Received	Thank You Sent	Number Attending

Guest List Planner

Name

Address

Telephone Number

E-mail Address

Gift

Save The Day Card Sent	Invitation Sent	R.S.V.P Received	Thank You Sent	Number Attending

Name

Address

Telephone Number

E-mail Address

Gift

Save The Day Card Sent	Invitation Sent	R.S.V.P Received	Thank You Sent	Number Attending

Name

Address

Telephone Number

E-mail Address

Gift

Save The Day Card Sent	Invitation Sent	R.S.V.P Received	Thank You Sent	Number Attending

Name

Address

Telephone Number

E-mail Address

Gift

Save The Day Card Sent	Invitation Sent	R.S.V.P Received	Thank You Sent	Number Attending

Name

Address

Telephone Number

E-mail Address

Gift

Save The Day Card Sent	Invitation Sent	R.S.V.P Received	Thank You Sent	Number Attending

Guest List Planner

Name

Address

Telephone Number

E-mail Address

Gift

Save The Day Card Sent	Invitation Sent	R.S.V.P Received	Thank You Sent	Number Attending

Name

Address

Telephone Number

E-mail Address

Gift

Save The Day Card Sent	Invitation Sent	R.S.V.P Received	Thank You Sent	Number Attending

Name

Address

Telephone Number

E-mail Address

Gift

Save The Day Card Sent	Invitation Sent	R.S.V.P Received	Thank You Sent	Number Attending

Name

Address

Telephone Number

E-mail Address

Gift

Save The Day Card Sent	Invitation Sent	R.S.V.P Received	Thank You Sent	Number Attending

Name

Address

Telephone Number

E-mail Address

Gift

Save The Day Card Sent	Invitation Sent	R.S.V.P Received	Thank You Sent	Number Attending

Guest List Planner

Name

Address

Telephone Number

E-mail Address

Gift

Save The Day Card Sent	Invitation Sent	R.S.V.P Received	Thank You Sent	Number Attending

Name

Address

Telephone Number

E-mail Address

Gift

Save The Day Card Sent	Invitation Sent	R.S.V.P Received	Thank You Sent	Number Attending

Name

Address

Telephone Number

E-mail Address

Gift

Save The Day Card Sent	Invitation Sent	R.S.V.P Received	Thank You Sent	Number Attending

Name

Address

Telephone Number

E-mail Address

Gift

Save The Day Card Sent	Invitation Sent	R.S.V.P Received	Thank You Sent	Number Attending

Name

Address

Telephone Number

E-mail Address

Gift

Save The Day Card Sent	Invitation Sent	R.S.V.P Received	Thank You Sent	Number Attending

Guest List Planner

Name

Address

Telephone Number

E-mail Address

Gift

Save The Day Card Sent	Invitation Sent	R.S.V.P Received	Thank You Sent	Number Attending

Name

Address

Telephone Number

E-mail Address

Gift

Save The Day Card Sent	Invitation Sent	R.S.V.P Received	Thank You Sent	Number Attending

Name

Address

Telephone Number

E-mail Address

Gift

Save The Day Card Sent	Invitation Sent	R.S.V.P Received	Thank You Sent	Number Attending

Name

Address

Telephone Number

E-mail Address

Gift

Save The Day Card Sent	Invitation Sent	R.S.V.P Received	Thank You Sent	Number Attending

Name

Address

Telephone Number

E-mail Address

Gift

Save The Day Card Sent	Invitation Sent	R.S.V.P Received	Thank You Sent	Number Attending

Guest List Planner

Name _____
Address _____
Telephone Number _____
E-mail Address _____
Gift _____

Save The Day Card Sent	Invitation Sent	R.S.V.P Received	Thank You Sent	Number Attending

Name _____
Address _____
Telephone Number _____
E-mail Address _____
Gift _____

Save The Day Card Sent	Invitation Sent	R.S.V.P Received	Thank You Sent	Number Attending

Name _____
Address _____
Telephone Number _____
E-mail Address _____
Gift _____

Save The Day Card Sent	Invitation Sent	R.S.V.P Received	Thank You Sent	Number Attending

Name _____
Address _____
Telephone Number _____
E-mail Address _____
Gift _____

Save The Day Card Sent	Invitation Sent	R.S.V.P Received	Thank You Sent	Number Attending

Name _____
Address _____
Telephone Number _____
E-mail Address _____
Gift _____

Save The Day Card Sent	Invitation Sent	R.S.V.P Received	Thank You Sent	Number Attending

Guest List Planner

Name

Address

Telephone Number

E-mail Address

Gift

Save The Day Card Sent	Invitation Sent	R.S.V.P Received	Thank You Sent	Number Attending

Name

Address

Telephone Number

E-mail Address

Gift

Save The Day Card Sent	Invitation Sent	R.S.V.P Received	Thank You Sent	Number Attending

Name

Address

Telephone Number

E-mail Address

Gift

Save The Day Card Sent	Invitation Sent	R.S.V.P Received	Thank You Sent	Number Attending

Name

Address

Telephone Number

E-mail Address

Gift

Save The Day Card Sent	Invitation Sent	R.S.V.P Received	Thank You Sent	Number Attending

Name

Address

Telephone Number

E-mail Address

Gift

Save The Day Card Sent	Invitation Sent	R.S.V.P Received	Thank You Sent	Number Attending

Guest List Planner

Name

Address

Telephone Number

E-mail Address

Gift

Save The Day Card Sent	Invitation Sent	R.S.V.P Received	Thank You Sent	Number Attending

Name

Address

Telephone Number

E-mail Address

Gift

Save The Day Card Sent	Invitation Sent	R.S.V.P Received	Thank You Sent	Number Attending

Name

Address

Telephone Number

E-mail Address

Gift

Save The Day Card Sent	Invitation Sent	R.S.V.P Received	Thank You Sent	Number Attending

Name

Address

Telephone Number

E-mail Address

Gift

Save The Day Card Sent	Invitation Sent	R.S.V.P Received	Thank You Sent	Number Attending

Name

Address

Telephone Number

E-mail Address

Gift

Save The Day Card Sent	Invitation Sent	R.S.V.P Received	Thank You Sent	Number Attending

Guest List Planner

Name

Address

Telephone Number

E-mail Address

Gift

Save The Day Card Sent	Invitation Sent	R.S.V.P Received	Thank You Sent	Number Attending

Name

Address

Telephone Number

E-mail Address

Gift

Save The Day Card Sent	Invitation Sent	R.S.V.P Received	Thank You Sent	Number Attending

Name

Address

Telephone Number

E-mail Address

Gift

Save The Day Card Sent	Invitation Sent	R.S.V.P Received	Thank You Sent	Number Attending

Name

Address

Telephone Number

E-mail Address

Gift

Save The Day Card Sent	Invitation Sent	R.S.V.P Received	Thank You Sent	Number Attending

Name

Address

Telephone Number

E-mail Address

Gift

Save The Day Card Sent	Invitation Sent	R.S.V.P Received	Thank You Sent	Number Attending

Guest List Planner

Name

Address

Telephone Number

E-mail Address

Gift

Save The Day Card Sent	Invitation Sent	R.S.V.P Received	Thank You Sent	Number Attending

Name

Address

Telephone Number

E-mail Address

Gift

Save The Day Card Sent	Invitation Sent	R.S.V.P Received	Thank You Sent	Number Attending

Name

Address

Telephone Number

E-mail Address

Gift

Save The Day Card Sent	Invitation Sent	R.S.V.P Received	Thank You Sent	Number Attending

Name

Address

Telephone Number

E-mail Address

Gift

Save The Day Card Sent	Invitation Sent	R.S.V.P Received	Thank You Sent	Number Attending

Name

Address

Telephone Number

E-mail Address

Gift

Save The Day Card Sent	Invitation Sent	R.S.V.P Received	Thank You Sent	Number Attending

Guest List Planner

Name

Address

Telephone Number

E-mail Address

Gift

Save The Day Card Sent	Invitation Sent	R.S.V.P Received	Thank You Sent	Number Attending

Name

Address

Telephone Number

E-mail Address

Gift

Save The Day Card Sent	Invitation Sent	R.S.V.P Received	Thank You Sent	Number Attending

Name

Address

Telephone Number

E-mail Address

Gift

Save The Day Card Sent	Invitation Sent	R.S.V.P Received	Thank You Sent	Number Attending

Name

Address

Telephone Number

E-mail Address

Gift

Save The Day Card Sent	Invitation Sent	R.S.V.P Received	Thank You Sent	Number Attending

Name

Address

Telephone Number

E-mail Address

Gift

Save The Day Card Sent	Invitation Sent	R.S.V.P Received	Thank You Sent	Number Attending

Guest List Planner

Name

Address

Telephone Number

E-mail Address

Gift

Save The Day Card Sent	Invitation Sent	R.S.V.P Received	Thank You Sent	Number Attending

Name

Address

Telephone Number

E-mail Address

Gift

Save The Day Card Sent	Invitation Sent	R.S.V.P Received	Thank You Sent	Number Attending

Name

Address

Telephone Number

E-mail Address

Gift

Save The Day Card Sent	Invitation Sent	R.S.V.P Received	Thank You Sent	Number Attending

Name

Address

Telephone Number

E-mail Address

Gift

Save The Day Card Sent	Invitation Sent	R.S.V.P Received	Thank You Sent	Number Attending

Name

Address

Telephone Number

E-mail Address

Gift

Save The Day Card Sent	Invitation Sent	R.S.V.P Received	Thank You Sent	Number Attending

Guest List Planner

Name

Address

Telephone Number

E-mail Address

Gift

Save The Day Card Sent	Invitation Sent	R.S.V.P Received	Thank You Sent	Number Attending

Name

Address

Telephone Number

E-mail Address

Gift

Save The Day Card Sent	Invitation Sent	R.S.V.P Received	Thank You Sent	Number Attending

Name

Address

Telephone Number

E-mail Address

Gift

Save The Day Card Sent	Invitation Sent	R.S.V.P Received	Thank You Sent	Number Attending

Name

Address

Telephone Number

E-mail Address

Gift

Save The Day Card Sent	Invitation Sent	R.S.V.P Received	Thank You Sent	Number Attending

Name

Address

Telephone Number

E-mail Address

Gift

Save The Day Card Sent	Invitation Sent	R.S.V.P Received	Thank You Sent	Number Attending

Guest List Planner

Name

Address

Telephone Number

E-mail Address

Gift

Save The Day Card Sent	Invitation Sent	R.S.V.P Received	Thank You Sent	Number Attending

Name

Address

Telephone Number

E-mail Address

Gift

Save The Day Card Sent	Invitation Sent	R.S.V.P Received	Thank You Sent	Number Attending

Name

Address

Telephone Number

E-mail Address

Gift

Save The Day Card Sent	Invitation Sent	R.S.V.P Received	Thank You Sent	Number Attending

Name

Address

Telephone Number

E-mail Address

Gift

Save The Day Card Sent	Invitation Sent	R.S.V.P Received	Thank You Sent	Number Attending

Name

Address

Telephone Number

E-mail Address

Gift

Save The Day Card Sent	Invitation Sent	R.S.V.P Received	Thank You Sent	Number Attending

Guest List Planner

Name

Address

Telephone Number

E-mail Address

Gift

Save The Day Card Sent	Invitation Sent	R.S.V.P Received	Thank You Sent	Number Attending

Name

Address

Telephone Number

E-mail Address

Gift

Save The Day Card Sent	Invitation Sent	R.S.V.P Received	Thank You Sent	Number Attending

Name

Address

Telephone Number

E-mail Address

Gift

Save The Day Card Sent	Invitation Sent	R.S.V.P Received	Thank You Sent	Number Attending

Name

Address

Telephone Number

E-mail Address

Gift

Save The Day Card Sent	Invitation Sent	R.S.V.P Received	Thank You Sent	Number Attending

Name

Address

Telephone Number

E-mail Address

Gift

Save The Day Card Sent	Invitation Sent	R.S.V.P Received	Thank You Sent	Number Attending

Guest List Planner

Name

Address

Telephone Number

E-mail Address

Gift

Save The Day Card Sent	Invitation Sent	R.S.V.P Received	Thank You Sent	Number Attending

Name

Address

Telephone Number

E-mail Address

Gift

Save The Day Card Sent	Invitation Sent	R.S.V.P Received	Thank You Sent	Number Attending

Name

Address

Telephone Number

E-mail Address

Gift

Save The Day Card Sent	Invitation Sent	R.S.V.P Received	Thank You Sent	Number Attending

Name

Address

Telephone Number

E-mail Address

Gift

Save The Day Card Sent	Invitation Sent	R.S.V.P Received	Thank You Sent	Number Attending

Name

Address

Telephone Number

E-mail Address

Gift

Save The Day Card Sent	Invitation Sent	R.S.V.P Received	Thank You Sent	Number Attending

Guest List Planner

Name

Address

Telephone Number

E-mail Address

Gift

Save The Day Card Sent	Invitation Sent	R.S.V.P Received	Thank You Sent	Number Attending

Name

Address

Telephone Number

E-mail Address

Gift

Save The Day Card Sent	Invitation Sent	R.S.V.P Received	Thank You Sent	Number Attending

Name

Address

Telephone Number

E-mail Address

Gift

Save The Day Card Sent	Invitation Sent	R.S.V.P Received	Thank You Sent	Number Attending

Name

Address

Telephone Number

E-mail Address

Gift

Save The Day Card Sent	Invitation Sent	R.S.V.P Received	Thank You Sent	Number Attending

Name

Address

Telephone Number

E-mail Address

Gift

Save The Day Card Sent	Invitation Sent	R.S.V.P Received	Thank You Sent	Number Attending

Guest List Planner

Name

Address

Telephone Number

E-mail Address

Gift

Save The Day Card Sent	Invitation Sent	R.S.V.P Received	Thank You Sent	Number Attending

Name

Address

Telephone Number

E-mail Address

Gift

Save The Day Card Sent	Invitation Sent	R.S.V.P Received	Thank You Sent	Number Attending

Name

Address

Telephone Number

E-mail Address

Gift

Save The Day Card Sent	Invitation Sent	R.S.V.P Received	Thank You Sent	Number Attending

Name

Address

Telephone Number

E-mail Address

Gift

Save The Day Card Sent	Invitation Sent	R.S.V.P Received	Thank You Sent	Number Attending

Name

Address

Telephone Number

E-mail Address

Gift

Save The Day Card Sent	Invitation Sent	R.S.V.P Received	Thank You Sent	Number Attending

Guest List Planner

Name

Address

Telephone Number

E-mail Address

Gift

Save The Day Card Sent	Invitation Sent	R.S.V.P Received	Thank You Sent	Number Attending

Name

Address

Telephone Number

E-mail Address

Gift

Save The Day Card Sent	Invitation Sent	R.S.V.P Received	Thank You Sent	Number Attending

Name

Address

Telephone Number

E-mail Address

Gift

Save The Day Card Sent	Invitation Sent	R.S.V.P Received	Thank You Sent	Number Attending

Name

Address

Telephone Number

E-mail Address

Gift

Save The Day Card Sent	Invitation Sent	R.S.V.P Received	Thank You Sent	Number Attending

Name

Address

Telephone Number

E-mail Address

Gift

Save The Day Card Sent	Invitation Sent	R.S.V.P Received	Thank You Sent	Number Attending

Guest List Planner

Name

Address

Telephone Number

E-mail Address

Gift

Save The Day Card Sent	Invitation Sent	R.S.V.P Received	Thank You Sent	Number Attending

Name

Address

Telephone Number

E-mail Address

Gift

Save The Day Card Sent	Invitation Sent	R.S.V.P Received	Thank You Sent	Number Attending

Name

Address

Telephone Number

E-mail Address

Gift

Save The Day Card Sent	Invitation Sent	R.S.V.P Received	Thank You Sent	Number Attending

Name

Address

Telephone Number

E-mail Address

Gift

Save The Day Card Sent	Invitation Sent	R.S.V.P Received	Thank You Sent	Number Attending

Name

Address

Telephone Number

E-mail Address

Gift

Save The Day Card Sent	Invitation Sent	R.S.V.P Received	Thank You Sent	Number Attending

Guest List Planner

Name

Address

Telephone Number

E-mail Address

Gift

Save The Day Card Sent	Invitation Sent	R.S.V.P Received	Thank You Sent	Number Attending

Name

Address

Telephone Number

E-mail Address

Gift

Save The Day Card Sent	Invitation Sent	R.S.V.P Received	Thank You Sent	Number Attending

Name

Address

Telephone Number

E-mail Address

Gift

Save The Day Card Sent	Invitation Sent	R.S.V.P Received	Thank You Sent	Number Attending

Name

Address

Telephone Number

E-mail Address

Gift

Save The Day Card Sent	Invitation Sent	R.S.V.P Received	Thank You Sent	Number Attending

Name

Address

Telephone Number

E-mail Address

Gift

Save The Day Card Sent	Invitation Sent	R.S.V.P Received	Thank You Sent	Number Attending

Guest List Planner

Name

Address

Telephone Number

E-mail Address

Gift

Save The Day Card Sent | Invitation Sent | R.S.V.P Received | Thank You Sent | Number Attending

Name

Address

Telephone Number

E-mail Address

Gift

Save The Day Card Sent | Invitation Sent | R.S.V.P Received | Thank You Sent | Number Attending

Name

Address

Telephone Number

E-mail Address

Gift

Save The Day Card Sent | Invitation Sent | R.S.V.P Received | Thank You Sent | Number Attending

Name

Address

Telephone Number

E-mail Address

Gift

Save The Day Card Sent | Invitation Sent | R.S.V.P Received | Thank You Sent | Number Attending

Name

Address

Telephone Number

E-mail Address

Gift

Save The Day Card Sent | Invitation Sent | R.S.V.P Received | Thank You Sent | Number Attending

Guest List Planner

Name

Address

Telephone Number

E-mail Address

Gift

Save The Day Card Sent	Invitation Sent	R.S.V.P Received	Thank You Sent	Number Attending

Name

Address

Telephone Number

E-mail Address

Gift

Save The Day Card Sent	Invitation Sent	R.S.V.P Received	Thank You Sent	Number Attending

Name

Address

Telephone Number

E-mail Address

Gift

Save The Day Card Sent	Invitation Sent	R.S.V.P Received	Thank You Sent	Number Attending

Name

Address

Telephone Number

E-mail Address

Gift

Save The Day Card Sent	Invitation Sent	R.S.V.P Received	Thank You Sent	Number Attending

Name

Address

Telephone Number

E-mail Address

Gift

Save The Day Card Sent	Invitation Sent	R.S.V.P Received	Thank You Sent	Number Attending

Guest List Planner

Name

Address

Telephone Number

E-mail Address

Gift

Save The Day Card Sent	Invitation Sent	R.S.V.P Received	Thank You Sent	Number Attending

Name

Address

Telephone Number

E-mail Address

Gift

Save The Day Card Sent	Invitation Sent	R.S.V.P Received	Thank You Sent	Number Attending

Name

Address

Telephone Number

E-mail Address

Gift

Save The Day Card Sent	Invitation Sent	R.S.V.P Received	Thank You Sent	Number Attending

Name

Address

Telephone Number

E-mail Address

Gift

Save The Day Card Sent	Invitation Sent	R.S.V.P Received	Thank You Sent	Number Attending

Name

Address

Telephone Number

E-mail Address

Gift

Save The Day Card Sent	Invitation Sent	R.S.V.P Received	Thank You Sent	Number Attending

Guest List Planner

Name

Address

Telephone Number

E-mail Address

Gift

| Save The Day Card Sent | Invitation Sent | R.S.V.P Received | Thank You Sent | Number Attending |

Name

Address

Telephone Number

E-mail Address

Gift

| Save The Day Card Sent | Invitation Sent | R.S.V.P Received | Thank You Sent | Number Attending |

Name

Address

Telephone Number

E-mail Address

Gift

| Save The Day Card Sent | Invitation Sent | R.S.V.P Received | Thank You Sent | Number Attending |

Name

Address

Telephone Number

E-mail Address

Gift

| Save The Day Card Sent | Invitation Sent | R.S.V.P Received | Thank You Sent | Number Attending |

Name

Address

Telephone Number

E-mail Address

Gift

| Save The Day Card Sent | Invitation Sent | R.S.V.P Received | Thank You Sent | Number Attending |

Guest List Planner

Name

Address

Telephone Number

E-mail Address

Gift

Save The Day Card Sent	Invitation Sent	R.S.V.P Received	Thank You Sent	Number Attending

Name

Address

Telephone Number

E-mail Address

Gift

Save The Day Card Sent	Invitation Sent	R.S.V.P Received	Thank You Sent	Number Attending

Name

Address

Telephone Number

E-mail Address

Gift

Save The Day Card Sent	Invitation Sent	R.S.V.P Received	Thank You Sent	Number Attending

Name

Address

Telephone Number

E-mail Address

Gift

Save The Day Card Sent	Invitation Sent	R.S.V.P Received	Thank You Sent	Number Attending

Name

Address

Telephone Number

E-mail Address

Gift

Save The Day Card Sent	Invitation Sent	R.S.V.P Received	Thank You Sent	Number Attending

Guest List Planner

Name

Address

Telephone Number

E-mail Address

Gift

Save The Day Card Sent	Invitation Sent	R.S.V.P Received	Thank You Sent	Number Attending

Name

Address

Telephone Number

E-mail Address

Gift

Save The Day Card Sent	Invitation Sent	R.S.V.P Received	Thank You Sent	Number Attending

Name

Address

Telephone Number

E-mail Address

Gift

Save The Day Card Sent	Invitation Sent	R.S.V.P Received	Thank You Sent	Number Attending

Name

Address

Telephone Number

E-mail Address

Gift

Save The Day Card Sent	Invitation Sent	R.S.V.P Received	Thank You Sent	Number Attending

Name

Address

Telephone Number

E-mail Address

Gift

Save The Day Card Sent	Invitation Sent	R.S.V.P Received	Thank You Sent	Number Attending

Guest List Planner

Name

Address

Telephone Number

E-mail Address

Gift

Save The Day Card Sent	Invitation Sent	R.S.V.P Received	Thank You Sent	Number Attending

Name

Address

Telephone Number

E-mail Address

Gift

Save The Day Card Sent	Invitation Sent	R.S.V.P Received	Thank You Sent	Number Attending

Name

Address

Telephone Number

E-mail Address

Gift

Save The Day Card Sent	Invitation Sent	R.S.V.P Received	Thank You Sent	Number Attending

Name

Address

Telephone Number

E-mail Address

Gift

Save The Day Card Sent	Invitation Sent	R.S.V.P Received	Thank You Sent	Number Attending

Name

Address

Telephone Number

E-mail Address

Gift

Save The Day Card Sent	Invitation Sent	R.S.V.P Received	Thank You Sent	Number Attending

Guest List Planner

Name

Address

Telephone Number

E-mail Address

Gift

Save The Day Card Sent	Invitation Sent	R.S.V.P Received	Thank You Sent	Number Attending

Name

Address

Telephone Number

E-mail Address

Gift

Save The Day Card Sent	Invitation Sent	R.S.V.P Received	Thank You Sent	Number Attending

Name

Address

Telephone Number

E-mail Address

Gift

Save The Day Card Sent	Invitation Sent	R.S.V.P Received	Thank You Sent	Number Attending

Name

Address

Telephone Number

E-mail Address

Gift

Save The Day Card Sent	Invitation Sent	R.S.V.P Received	Thank You Sent	Number Attending

Name

Address

Telephone Number

E-mail Address

Gift

Save The Day Card Sent	Invitation Sent	R.S.V.P Received	Thank You Sent	Number Attending

Guest List Planner

Name
_____
Address
_____
Telephone Number
_____
E-mail Address
_____
Gift
_____

Save The Day Card Sent	Invitation Sent	R.S.V.P Received	Thank You Sent	Number Attending

Name
_____
Address
_____
Telephone Number
_____
E-mail Address
_____
Gift
_____

Save The Day Card Sent	Invitation Sent	R.S.V.P Received	Thank You Sent	Number Attending

Name
_____
Address
_____
Telephone Number
_____
E-mail Address
_____
Gift
_____

Save The Day Card Sent	Invitation Sent	R.S.V.P Received	Thank You Sent	Number Attending

Name
_____
Address
_____
Telephone Number
_____
E-mail Address
_____
Gift
_____

Save The Day Card Sent	Invitation Sent	R.S.V.P Received	Thank You Sent	Number Attending

Name
_____
Address
_____
Telephone Number
_____
E-mail Address
_____
Gift
_____

Save The Day Card Sent	Invitation Sent	R.S.V.P Received	Thank You Sent	Number Attending

Guest List Planner

Name

Address

Telephone Number

E-mail Address

Gift

| Save The Day Card Sent | Invitation Sent | R.S.V.P Received | Thank You Sent | Number Attending |

Name

Address

Telephone Number

E-mail Address

Gift

| Save The Day Card Sent | Invitation Sent | R.S.V.P Received | Thank You Sent | Number Attending |

Name

Address

Telephone Number

E-mail Address

Gift

| Save The Day Card Sent | Invitation Sent | R.S.V.P Received | Thank You Sent | Number Attending |

Name

Address

Telephone Number

E-mail Address

Gift

| Save The Day Card Sent | Invitation Sent | R.S.V.P Received | Thank You Sent | Number Attending |

Name

Address

Telephone Number

E-mail Address

Gift

| Save The Day Card Sent | Invitation Sent | R.S.V.P Received | Thank You Sent | Number Attending |

Guest List Planner

Name

Address

Telephone Number

E-mail Address

Gift

Save The Day Card Sent	Invitation Sent	R.S.V.P Received	Thank You Sent	Number Attending

Name

Address

Telephone Number

E-mail Address

Gift

Save The Day Card Sent	Invitation Sent	R.S.V.P Received	Thank You Sent	Number Attending

Name

Address

Telephone Number

E-mail Address

Gift

Save The Day Card Sent	Invitation Sent	R.S.V.P Received	Thank You Sent	Number Attending

Name

Address

Telephone Number

E-mail Address

Gift

Save The Day Card Sent	Invitation Sent	R.S.V.P Received	Thank You Sent	Number Attending

Name

Address

Telephone Number

E-mail Address

Gift

Save The Day Card Sent	Invitation Sent	R.S.V.P Received	Thank You Sent	Number Attending

Guest List Planner

Name

Address

Telephone Number

E-mail Address

Gift

Save The Day Card Sent	Invitation Sent	R.S.V.P Received	Thank You Sent	Number Attending

Name

Address

Telephone Number

E-mail Address

Gift

Save The Day Card Sent	Invitation Sent	R.S.V.P Received	Thank You Sent	Number Attending

Name

Address

Telephone Number

E-mail Address

Gift

Save The Day Card Sent	Invitation Sent	R.S.V.P Received	Thank You Sent	Number Attending

Name

Address

Telephone Number

E-mail Address

Gift

Save The Day Card Sent	Invitation Sent	R.S.V.P Received	Thank You Sent	Number Attending

Name

Address

Telephone Number

E-mail Address

Gift

Save The Day Card Sent	Invitation Sent	R.S.V.P Received	Thank You Sent	Number Attending

Guest List Planner

Name

Address

Telephone Number

E-mail Address

Gift

| Save The Day Card Sent | Invitation Sent | R.S.V.P Received | Thank You Sent | Number Attending |

Name

Address

Telephone Number

E-mail Address

Gift

| Save The Day Card Sent | Invitation Sent | R.S.V.P Received | Thank You Sent | Number Attending |

Name

Address

Telephone Number

E-mail Address

Gift

| Save The Day Card Sent | Invitation Sent | R.S.V.P Received | Thank You Sent | Number Attending |

Name

Address

Telephone Number

E-mail Address

Gift

| Save The Day Card Sent | Invitation Sent | R.S.V.P Received | Thank You Sent | Number Attending |

Name

Address

Telephone Number

E-mail Address

Gift

| Save The Day Card Sent | Invitation Sent | R.S.V.P Received | Thank You Sent | Number Attending |

Guest List Planner

Name

Address

Telephone Number

E-mail Address

Gift

Save The Day Card Sent	Invitation Sent	R.S.V.P Received	Thank You Sent	Number Attending

Name

Address

Telephone Number

E-mail Address

Gift

Save The Day Card Sent	Invitation Sent	R.S.V.P Received	Thank You Sent	Number Attending

Name

Address

Telephone Number

E-mail Address

Gift

Save The Day Card Sent	Invitation Sent	R.S.V.P Received	Thank You Sent	Number Attending

Name

Address

Telephone Number

E-mail Address

Gift

Save The Day Card Sent	Invitation Sent	R.S.V.P Received	Thank You Sent	Number Attending

Name

Address

Telephone Number

E-mail Address

Gift

Save The Day Card Sent	Invitation Sent	R.S.V.P Received	Thank You Sent	Number Attending

Guest List Planner

Name _____
Address _____
Telephone Number _____
E-mail Address _____
Gift _____

Save The Day Card Sent	Invitation Sent	R.S.V.P Received	Thank You Sent	Number Attending

Name _____
Address _____
Telephone Number _____
E-mail Address _____
Gift _____

Save The Day Card Sent	Invitation Sent	R.S.V.P Received	Thank You Sent	Number Attending

Name _____
Address _____
Telephone Number _____
E-mail Address _____
Gift _____

Save The Day Card Sent	Invitation Sent	R.S.V.P Received	Thank You Sent	Number Attending

Name _____
Address _____
Telephone Number _____
E-mail Address _____
Gift _____

Save The Day Card Sent	Invitation Sent	R.S.V.P Received	Thank You Sent	Number Attending

Name _____
Address _____
Telephone Number _____
E-mail Address _____
Gift _____

Save The Day Card Sent	Invitation Sent	R.S.V.P Received	Thank You Sent	Number Attending

Guest List Planner

Name

Address

Telephone Number

E-mail Address

Gift

Save The Day Card Sent	Invitation Sent	R.S.V.P Received	Thank You Sent	Number Attending

Name

Address

Telephone Number

E-mail Address

Gift

Save The Day Card Sent	Invitation Sent	R.S.V.P Received	Thank You Sent	Number Attending

Name

Address

Telephone Number

E-mail Address

Gift

Save The Day Card Sent	Invitation Sent	R.S.V.P Received	Thank You Sent	Number Attending

Name

Address

Telephone Number

E-mail Address

Gift

Save The Day Card Sent	Invitation Sent	R.S.V.P Received	Thank You Sent	Number Attending

Name

Address

Telephone Number

E-mail Address

Gift

Save The Day Card Sent	Invitation Sent	R.S.V.P Received	Thank You Sent	Number Attending

Guest List Planner

Name

Address

Telephone Number

E-mail Address

Gift

Save The Day Card Sent	Invitation Sent	R.S.V.P Received	Thank You Sent	Number Attending

Name

Address

Telephone Number

E-mail Address

Gift

Save The Day Card Sent	Invitation Sent	R.S.V.P Received	Thank You Sent	Number Attending

Name

Address

Telephone Number

E-mail Address

Gift

Save The Day Card Sent	Invitation Sent	R.S.V.P Received	Thank You Sent	Number Attending

Name

Address

Telephone Number

E-mail Address

Gift

Save The Day Card Sent	Invitation Sent	R.S.V.P Received	Thank You Sent	Number Attending

Name

Address

Telephone Number

E-mail Address

Gift

Save The Day Card Sent	Invitation Sent	R.S.V.P Received	Thank You Sent	Number Attending

Guest List Planner

Name

Address

Telephone Number

E-mail Address

Gift

Save The Day Card Sent	Invitation Sent	R.S.V.P Received	Thank You Sent	Number Attending

Name

Address

Telephone Number

E-mail Address

Gift

Save The Day Card Sent	Invitation Sent	R.S.V.P Received	Thank You Sent	Number Attending

Name

Address

Telephone Number

E-mail Address

Gift

Save The Day Card Sent	Invitation Sent	R.S.V.P Received	Thank You Sent	Number Attending

Name

Address

Telephone Number

E-mail Address

Gift

Save The Day Card Sent	Invitation Sent	R.S.V.P Received	Thank You Sent	Number Attending

Name

Address

Telephone Number

E-mail Address

Gift

Save The Day Card Sent	Invitation Sent	R.S.V.P Received	Thank You Sent	Number Attending

Guest List Planner

Name

Address

Telephone Number

E-mail Address

Gift

Save The Day Card Sent | Invitation Sent | R.S.V.P Received | Thank You Sent | Number Attending

Name

Address

Telephone Number

E-mail Address

Gift

Save The Day Card Sent | Invitation Sent | R.S.V.P Received | Thank You Sent | Number Attending

Name

Address

Telephone Number

E-mail Address

Gift

Save The Day Card Sent | Invitation Sent | R.S.V.P Received | Thank You Sent | Number Attending

Name

Address

Telephone Number

E-mail Address

Gift

Save The Day Card Sent | Invitation Sent | R.S.V.P Received | Thank You Sent | Number Attending

Name

Address

Telephone Number

E-mail Address

Gift

Save The Day Card Sent | Invitation Sent | R.S.V.P Received | Thank You Sent | Number Attending

Guest List Planner

Name

Address

Telephone Number

E-mail Address

Gift

Save The Day Card Sent	Invitation Sent	R.S.V.P Received	Thank You Sent	Number Attending

Name

Address

Telephone Number

E-mail Address

Gift

Save The Day Card Sent	Invitation Sent	R.S.V.P Received	Thank You Sent	Number Attending

Name

Address

Telephone Number

E-mail Address

Gift

Save The Day Card Sent	Invitation Sent	R.S.V.P Received	Thank You Sent	Number Attending

Name

Address

Telephone Number

E-mail Address

Gift

Save The Day Card Sent	Invitation Sent	R.S.V.P Received	Thank You Sent	Number Attending

Name

Address

Telephone Number

E-mail Address

Gift

Save The Day Card Sent	Invitation Sent	R.S.V.P Received	Thank You Sent	Number Attending

Guest List Planner

Name

Address

Telephone Number

E-mail Address

Gift

Save The Day Card Sent	Invitation Sent	R.S.V.P Received	Thank You Sent	Number Attending

Name

Address

Telephone Number

E-mail Address

Gift

Save The Day Card Sent	Invitation Sent	R.S.V.P Received	Thank You Sent	Number Attending

Name

Address

Telephone Number

E-mail Address

Gift

Save The Day Card Sent	Invitation Sent	R.S.V.P Received	Thank You Sent	Number Attending

Name

Address

Telephone Number

E-mail Address

Gift

Save The Day Card Sent	Invitation Sent	R.S.V.P Received	Thank You Sent	Number Attending

Name

Address

Telephone Number

E-mail Address

Gift

Save The Day Card Sent	Invitation Sent	R.S.V.P Received	Thank You Sent	Number Attending

Guest List Planner

Name

Address

Telephone Number

E-mail Address

Gift

Save The Day Card Sent	Invitation Sent	R.S.V.P Received	Thank You Sent	Number Attending

Name

Address

Telephone Number

E-mail Address

Gift

Save The Day Card Sent	Invitation Sent	R.S.V.P Received	Thank You Sent	Number Attending

Name

Address

Telephone Number

E-mail Address

Gift

Save The Day Card Sent	Invitation Sent	R.S.V.P Received	Thank You Sent	Number Attending

Name

Address

Telephone Number

E-mail Address

Gift

Save The Day Card Sent	Invitation Sent	R.S.V.P Received	Thank You Sent	Number Attending

Name

Address

Telephone Number

E-mail Address

Gift

Save The Day Card Sent	Invitation Sent	R.S.V.P Received	Thank You Sent	Number Attending

Guest List Planner

Name
___

Address
___

Telephone Number
___

E-mail Address
___

Gift
___

Save The Day Card Sent	Invitation Sent	R.S.V.P Received	Thank You Sent	Number Attending

Name
___

Address
___

Telephone Number
___

E-mail Address
___

Gift
___

Save The Day Card Sent	Invitation Sent	R.S.V.P Received	Thank You Sent	Number Attending

Name
___

Address
___

Telephone Number
___

E-mail Address
___

Gift
___

Save The Day Card Sent	Invitation Sent	R.S.V.P Received	Thank You Sent	Number Attending

Name
___

Address
___

Telephone Number
___

E-mail Address
___

Gift
___

Save The Day Card Sent	Invitation Sent	R.S.V.P Received	Thank You Sent	Number Attending

Name
___

Address
___

Telephone Number
___

E-mail Address
___

Gift
___

Save The Day Card Sent	Invitation Sent	R.S.V.P Received	Thank You Sent	Number Attending

Guest List Planner

Name

Address

Telephone Number

E-mail Address

Gift

Save The Day Card Sent	Invitation Sent	R.S.V.P Received	Thank You Sent	Number Attending

Name

Address

Telephone Number

E-mail Address

Gift

Save The Day Card Sent	Invitation Sent	R.S.V.P Received	Thank You Sent	Number Attending

Name

Address

Telephone Number

E-mail Address

Gift

Save The Day Card Sent	Invitation Sent	R.S.V.P Received	Thank You Sent	Number Attending

Name

Address

Telephone Number

E-mail Address

Gift

Save The Day Card Sent	Invitation Sent	R.S.V.P Received	Thank You Sent	Number Attending

Name

Address

Telephone Number

E-mail Address

Gift

Save The Day Card Sent	Invitation Sent	R.S.V.P Received	Thank You Sent	Number Attending

Guest List Planner

Name

Address

Telephone Number

E-mail Address

Gift

Save The Day Card Sent	Invitation Sent	R.S.V.P Received	Thank You Sent	Number Attending

Name

Address

Telephone Number

E-mail Address

Gift

Save The Day Card Sent	Invitation Sent	R.S.V.P Received	Thank You Sent	Number Attending

Name

Address

Telephone Number

E-mail Address

Gift

Save The Day Card Sent	Invitation Sent	R.S.V.P Received	Thank You Sent	Number Attending

Name

Address

Telephone Number

E-mail Address

Gift

Save The Day Card Sent	Invitation Sent	R.S.V.P Received	Thank You Sent	Number Attending

Name

Address

Telephone Number

E-mail Address

Gift

Save The Day Card Sent	Invitation Sent	R.S.V.P Received	Thank You Sent	Number Attending

Guest List Planner

Name

Address

Telephone Number

E-mail Address

Gift

Save The Day Card Sent	Invitation Sent	R.S.V.P Received	Thank You Sent	Number Attending

Name

Address

Telephone Number

E-mail Address

Gift

Save The Day Card Sent	Invitation Sent	R.S.V.P Received	Thank You Sent	Number Attending

Name

Address

Telephone Number

E-mail Address

Gift

Save The Day Card Sent	Invitation Sent	R.S.V.P Received	Thank You Sent	Number Attending

Name

Address

Telephone Number

E-mail Address

Gift

Save The Day Card Sent	Invitation Sent	R.S.V.P Received	Thank You Sent	Number Attending

Name

Address

Telephone Number

E-mail Address

Gift

Save The Day Card Sent	Invitation Sent	R.S.V.P Received	Thank You Sent	Number Attending

Guest List Planner

Name

Address

Telephone Number

E-mail Address

Gift

| Save The Day Card Sent | Invitation Sent | R.S.V.P Received | Thank You Sent | Number Attending |

Name

Address

Telephone Number

E-mail Address

Gift

| Save The Day Card Sent | Invitation Sent | R.S.V.P Received | Thank You Sent | Number Attending |

Name

Address

Telephone Number

E-mail Address

Gift

| Save The Day Card Sent | Invitation Sent | R.S.V.P Received | Thank You Sent | Number Attending |

Name

Address

Telephone Number

E-mail Address

Gift

| Save The Day Card Sent | Invitation Sent | R.S.V.P Received | Thank You Sent | Number Attending |

Name

Address

Telephone Number

E-mail Address

Gift

| Save The Day Card Sent | Invitation Sent | R.S.V.P Received | Thank You Sent | Number Attending |

Guest List Planner

Name

Address

Telephone Number

E-mail Address

Gift

Save The Day Card Sent	Invitation Sent	R.S.V.P Received	Thank You Sent	Number Attending

Name

Address

Telephone Number

E-mail Address

Gift

Save The Day Card Sent	Invitation Sent	R.S.V.P Received	Thank You Sent	Number Attending

Name

Address

Telephone Number

E-mail Address

Gift

Save The Day Card Sent	Invitation Sent	R.S.V.P Received	Thank You Sent	Number Attending

Name

Address

Telephone Number

E-mail Address

Gift

Save The Day Card Sent	Invitation Sent	R.S.V.P Received	Thank You Sent	Number Attending

Name

Address

Telephone Number

E-mail Address

Gift

Save The Day Card Sent	Invitation Sent	R.S.V.P Received	Thank You Sent	Number Attending

Guest List Planner

Name

Address

Telephone Number

E-mail Address

Gift

| Save The Day Card Sent | Invitation Sent | R.S.V.P Received | Thank You Sent | Number Attending |

Name

Address

Telephone Number

E-mail Address

Gift

| Save The Day Card Sent | Invitation Sent | R.S.V.P Received | Thank You Sent | Number Attending |

Name

Address

Telephone Number

E-mail Address

Gift

| Save The Day Card Sent | Invitation Sent | R.S.V.P Received | Thank You Sent | Number Attending |

Name

Address

Telephone Number

E-mail Address

Gift

| Save The Day Card Sent | Invitation Sent | R.S.V.P Received | Thank You Sent | Number Attending |

Name

Address

Telephone Number

E-mail Address

Gift

| Save The Day Card Sent | Invitation Sent | R.S.V.P Received | Thank You Sent | Number Attending |

Guest List Planner

Name

Address

Telephone Number

E-mail Address

Gift

Save The Day Card Sent	Invitation Sent	R.S.V.P Received	Thank You Sent	Number Attending

Name

Address

Telephone Number

E-mail Address

Gift

Save The Day Card Sent	Invitation Sent	R.S.V.P Received	Thank You Sent	Number Attending

Name

Address

Telephone Number

E-mail Address

Gift

Save The Day Card Sent	Invitation Sent	R.S.V.P Received	Thank You Sent	Number Attending

Name

Address

Telephone Number

E-mail Address

Gift

Save The Day Card Sent	Invitation Sent	R.S.V.P Received	Thank You Sent	Number Attending

Name

Address

Telephone Number

E-mail Address

Gift

Save The Day Card Sent	Invitation Sent	R.S.V.P Received	Thank You Sent	Number Attending

Guest List Planner

Name

Address

Telephone Number

E-mail Address

Gift

Save The Day Card Sent | Invitation Sent | R.S.V.P Received | Thank You Sent | Number Attending

Name

Address

Telephone Number

E-mail Address

Gift

Save The Day Card Sent | Invitation Sent | R.S.V.P Received | Thank You Sent | Number Attending

Name

Address

Telephone Number

E-mail Address

Gift

Save The Day Card Sent | Invitation Sent | R.S.V.P Received | Thank You Sent | Number Attending

Name

Address

Telephone Number

E-mail Address

Gift

Save The Day Card Sent | Invitation Sent | R.S.V.P Received | Thank You Sent | Number Attending

Name

Address

Telephone Number

E-mail Address

Gift

Save The Day Card Sent | Invitation Sent | R.S.V.P Received | Thank You Sent | Number Attending

Guest List Planner

Name

Address

Telephone Number

E-mail Address

Gift

Save The Day Card Sent	Invitation Sent	R.S.V.P Received	Thank You Sent	Number Attending

Name

Address

Telephone Number

E-mail Address

Gift

Save The Day Card Sent	Invitation Sent	R.S.V.P Received	Thank You Sent	Number Attending

Name

Address

Telephone Number

E-mail Address

Gift

Save The Day Card Sent	Invitation Sent	R.S.V.P Received	Thank You Sent	Number Attending

Name

Address

Telephone Number

E-mail Address

Gift

Save The Day Card Sent	Invitation Sent	R.S.V.P Received	Thank You Sent	Number Attending

Name

Address

Telephone Number

E-mail Address

Gift

Save The Day Card Sent	Invitation Sent	R.S.V.P Received	Thank You Sent	Number Attending

Guest List Planner

Name

Address

Telephone Number

E-mail Address

Gift

Save The Day Card Sent	Invitation Sent	R.S.V.P Received	Thank You Sent	Number Attending

Name

Address

Telephone Number

E-mail Address

Gift

Save The Day Card Sent	Invitation Sent	R.S.V.P Received	Thank You Sent	Number Attending

Name

Address

Telephone Number

E-mail Address

Gift

Save The Day Card Sent	Invitation Sent	R.S.V.P Received	Thank You Sent	Number Attending

Name

Address

Telephone Number

E-mail Address

Gift

Save The Day Card Sent	Invitation Sent	R.S.V.P Received	Thank You Sent	Number Attending

Name

Address

Telephone Number

E-mail Address

Gift

Save The Day Card Sent	Invitation Sent	R.S.V.P Received	Thank You Sent	Number Attending

Guest List Planner

Name

Address

Telephone Number

E-mail Address

Gift

Save The Day Card Sent	Invitation Sent	R.S.V.P Received	Thank You Sent	Number Attending

Name

Address

Telephone Number

E-mail Address

Gift

Save The Day Card Sent	Invitation Sent	R.S.V.P Received	Thank You Sent	Number Attending

Name

Address

Telephone Number

E-mail Address

Gift

Save The Day Card Sent	Invitation Sent	R.S.V.P Received	Thank You Sent	Number Attending

Name

Address

Telephone Number

E-mail Address

Gift

Save The Day Card Sent	Invitation Sent	R.S.V.P Received	Thank You Sent	Number Attending

Name

Address

Telephone Number

E-mail Address

Gift

Save The Day Card Sent	Invitation Sent	R.S.V.P Received	Thank You Sent	Number Attending

Guest List Planner

Name

Address

Telephone Number

E-mail Address

Gift

Save The Day Card Sent	Invitation Sent	R.S.V.P Received	Thank You Sent	Number Attending

Name

Address

Telephone Number

E-mail Address

Gift

Save The Day Card Sent	Invitation Sent	R.S.V.P Received	Thank You Sent	Number Attending

Name

Address

Telephone Number

E-mail Address

Gift

Save The Day Card Sent	Invitation Sent	R.S.V.P Received	Thank You Sent	Number Attending

Name

Address

Telephone Number

E-mail Address

Gift

Save The Day Card Sent	Invitation Sent	R.S.V.P Received	Thank You Sent	Number Attending

Name

Address

Telephone Number

E-mail Address

Gift

Save The Day Card Sent	Invitation Sent	R.S.V.P Received	Thank You Sent	Number Attending

Guest List Planner

Name

Address

Telephone Number

E-mail Address

Gift

Save The Day Card Sent	Invitation Sent	R.S.V.P Received	Thank You Sent	Number Attending

Name

Address

Telephone Number

E-mail Address

Gift

Save The Day Card Sent	Invitation Sent	R.S.V.P Received	Thank You Sent	Number Attending

Name

Address

Telephone Number

E-mail Address

Gift

Save The Day Card Sent	Invitation Sent	R.S.V.P Received	Thank You Sent	Number Attending

Name

Address

Telephone Number

E-mail Address

Gift

Save The Day Card Sent	Invitation Sent	R.S.V.P Received	Thank You Sent	Number Attending

Name

Address

Telephone Number

E-mail Address

Gift

Save The Day Card Sent	Invitation Sent	R.S.V.P Received	Thank You Sent	Number Attending

Guest List Planner

Name

Address

Telephone Number

E-mail Address

Gift

Save The Day Card Sent	Invitation Sent	R.S.V.P Received	Thank You Sent	Number Attending

Name

Address

Telephone Number

E-mail Address

Gift

Save The Day Card Sent	Invitation Sent	R.S.V.P Received	Thank You Sent	Number Attending

Name

Address

Telephone Number

E-mail Address

Gift

Save The Day Card Sent	Invitation Sent	R.S.V.P Received	Thank You Sent	Number Attending

Name

Address

Telephone Number

E-mail Address

Gift

Save The Day Card Sent	Invitation Sent	R.S.V.P Received	Thank You Sent	Number Attending

Name

Address

Telephone Number

E-mail Address

Gift

Save The Day Card Sent	Invitation Sent	R.S.V.P Received	Thank You Sent	Number Attending

Guest List Planner

Name

Address

Telephone Number

E-mail Address

Gift

Save The Day Card Sent	Invitation Sent	R.S.V.P Received	Thank You Sent	Number Attending

Name

Address

Telephone Number

E-mail Address

Gift

Save The Day Card Sent	Invitation Sent	R.S.V.P Received	Thank You Sent	Number Attending

Name

Address

Telephone Number

E-mail Address

Gift

Save The Day Card Sent	Invitation Sent	R.S.V.P Received	Thank You Sent	Number Attending

Name

Address

Telephone Number

E-mail Address

Gift

Save The Day Card Sent	Invitation Sent	R.S.V.P Received	Thank You Sent	Number Attending

Name

Address

Telephone Number

E-mail Address

Gift

Save The Day Card Sent	Invitation Sent	R.S.V.P Received	Thank You Sent	Number Attending

Guest List Planner

Name

Address

Telephone Number

E-mail Address

Gift

| Save The Day Card Sent | Invitation Sent | R.S.V.P Received | Thank You Sent | Number Attending |

Name

Address

Telephone Number

E-mail Address

Gift

| Save The Day Card Sent | Invitation Sent | R.S.V.P Received | Thank You Sent | Number Attending |

Name

Address

Telephone Number

E-mail Address

Gift

| Save The Day Card Sent | Invitation Sent | R.S.V.P Received | Thank You Sent | Number Attending |

Name

Address

Telephone Number

E-mail Address

Gift

| Save The Day Card Sent | Invitation Sent | R.S.V.P Received | Thank You Sent | Number Attending |

Name

Address

Telephone Number

E-mail Address

Gift

| Save The Day Card Sent | Invitation Sent | R.S.V.P Received | Thank You Sent | Number Attending |

Guest List Planner

Name

Address

Telephone Number

E-mail Address

Gift

Save The Day Card Sent	Invitation Sent	R.S.V.P Received	Thank You Sent	Number Attending

Name

Address

Telephone Number

E-mail Address

Gift

Save The Day Card Sent	Invitation Sent	R.S.V.P Received	Thank You Sent	Number Attending

Name

Address

Telephone Number

E-mail Address

Gift

Save The Day Card Sent	Invitation Sent	R.S.V.P Received	Thank You Sent	Number Attending

Name

Address

Telephone Number

E-mail Address

Gift

Save The Day Card Sent	Invitation Sent	R.S.V.P Received	Thank You Sent	Number Attending

Name

Address

Telephone Number

E-mail Address

Gift

Save The Day Card Sent	Invitation Sent	R.S.V.P Received	Thank You Sent	Number Attending

Guest List Planner

Name

Address

Telephone Number

E-mail Address

Gift

Save The Day Card Sent	Invitation Sent	R.S.V.P Received	Thank You Sent	Number Attending

Name

Address

Telephone Number

E-mail Address

Gift

Save The Day Card Sent	Invitation Sent	R.S.V.P Received	Thank You Sent	Number Attending

Name

Address

Telephone Number

E-mail Address

Gift

Save The Day Card Sent	Invitation Sent	R.S.V.P Received	Thank You Sent	Number Attending

Name

Address

Telephone Number

E-mail Address

Gift

Save The Day Card Sent	Invitation Sent	R.S.V.P Received	Thank You Sent	Number Attending

Name

Address

Telephone Number

E-mail Address

Gift

Save The Day Card Sent	Invitation Sent	R.S.V.P Received	Thank You Sent	Number Attending

Guest List Planner

Name

Address

Telephone Number

E-mail Address

Gift

| Save The Day Card Sent | Invitation Sent | R.S.V.P Received | Thank You Sent | Number Attending |

Name

Address

Telephone Number

E-mail Address

Gift

| Save The Day Card Sent | Invitation Sent | R.S.V.P Received | Thank You Sent | Number Attending |

Name

Address

Telephone Number

E-mail Address

Gift

| Save The Day Card Sent | Invitation Sent | R.S.V.P Received | Thank You Sent | Number Attending |

Name

Address

Telephone Number

E-mail Address

Gift

| Save The Day Card Sent | Invitation Sent | R.S.V.P Received | Thank You Sent | Number Attending |

Name

Address

Telephone Number

E-mail Address

Gift

| Save The Day Card Sent | Invitation Sent | R.S.V.P Received | Thank You Sent | Number Attending |

Guest List Planner

Name

Address

Telephone Number

E-mail Address

Gift

Save The Day Card Sent	Invitation Sent	R.S.V.P Received	Thank You Sent	Number Attending

Name

Address

Telephone Number

E-mail Address

Gift

Save The Day Card Sent	Invitation Sent	R.S.V.P Received	Thank You Sent	Number Attending

Name

Address

Telephone Number

E-mail Address

Gift

Save The Day Card Sent	Invitation Sent	R.S.V.P Received	Thank You Sent	Number Attending

Name

Address

Telephone Number

E-mail Address

Gift

Save The Day Card Sent	Invitation Sent	R.S.V.P Received	Thank You Sent	Number Attending

Name

Address

Telephone Number

E-mail Address

Gift

Save The Day Card Sent	Invitation Sent	R.S.V.P Received	Thank You Sent	Number Attending

Guest List Planner

Name

Address

Telephone Number

E-mail Address

Gift

Save The Day Card Sent	Invitation Sent	R.S.V.P Received	Thank You Sent	Number Attending

Name

Address

Telephone Number

E-mail Address

Gift

Save The Day Card Sent	Invitation Sent	R.S.V.P Received	Thank You Sent	Number Attending

Name

Address

Telephone Number

E-mail Address

Gift

Save The Day Card Sent	Invitation Sent	R.S.V.P Received	Thank You Sent	Number Attending

Name

Address

Telephone Number

E-mail Address

Gift

Save The Day Card Sent	Invitation Sent	R.S.V.P Received	Thank You Sent	Number Attending

Name

Address

Telephone Number

E-mail Address

Gift

Save The Day Card Sent	Invitation Sent	R.S.V.P Received	Thank You Sent	Number Attending

Guest List Planner

Name

Address

Telephone Number

E-mail Address

Gift

| Save The Day Card Sent | Invitation Sent | R.S.V.P Received | Thank You Sent | Number Attending |

Name

Address

Telephone Number

E-mail Address

Gift

| Save The Day Card Sent | Invitation Sent | R.S.V.P Received | Thank You Sent | Number Attending |

Name

Address

Telephone Number

E-mail Address

Gift

| Save The Day Card Sent | Invitation Sent | R.S.V.P Received | Thank You Sent | Number Attending |

Name

Address

Telephone Number

E-mail Address

Gift

| Save The Day Card Sent | Invitation Sent | R.S.V.P Received | Thank You Sent | Number Attending |

Name

Address

Telephone Number

E-mail Address

Gift

| Save The Day Card Sent | Invitation Sent | R.S.V.P Received | Thank You Sent | Number Attending |

Guest List Planner

Name

Address

Telephone Number

E-mail Address

Gift

Save The Day Card Sent	Invitation Sent	R.S.V.P Received	Thank You Sent	Number Attending

Name

Address

Telephone Number

E-mail Address

Gift

Save The Day Card Sent	Invitation Sent	R.S.V.P Received	Thank You Sent	Number Attending

Name

Address

Telephone Number

E-mail Address

Gift

Save The Day Card Sent	Invitation Sent	R.S.V.P Received	Thank You Sent	Number Attending

Name

Address

Telephone Number

E-mail Address

Gift

Save The Day Card Sent	Invitation Sent	R.S.V.P Received	Thank You Sent	Number Attending

Name

Address

Telephone Number

E-mail Address

Gift

Save The Day Card Sent	Invitation Sent	R.S.V.P Received	Thank You Sent	Number Attending

Guest List Planner

Name

Address

Telephone Number

E-mail Address

Gift

Save The Day Card Sent	Invitation Sent	R.S.V.P Received	Thank You Sent	Number Attending

Name

Address

Telephone Number

E-mail Address

Gift

Save The Day Card Sent	Invitation Sent	R.S.V.P Received	Thank You Sent	Number Attending

Name

Address

Telephone Number

E-mail Address

Gift

Save The Day Card Sent	Invitation Sent	R.S.V.P Received	Thank You Sent	Number Attending

Name

Address

Telephone Number

E-mail Address

Gift

Save The Day Card Sent	Invitation Sent	R.S.V.P Received	Thank You Sent	Number Attending

Name

Address

Telephone Number

E-mail Address

Gift

Save The Day Card Sent	Invitation Sent	R.S.V.P Received	Thank You Sent	Number Attending

Guest List Planner

Name

Address

Telephone Number

E-mail Address

Gift

Save The Day Card Sent	Invitation Sent	R.S.V.P Received	Thank You Sent	Number Attending

Name

Address

Telephone Number

E-mail Address

Gift

Save The Day Card Sent	Invitation Sent	R.S.V.P Received	Thank You Sent	Number Attending

Name

Address

Telephone Number

E-mail Address

Gift

Save The Day Card Sent	Invitation Sent	R.S.V.P Received	Thank You Sent	Number Attending

Name

Address

Telephone Number

E-mail Address

Gift

Save The Day Card Sent	Invitation Sent	R.S.V.P Received	Thank You Sent	Number Attending

Name

Address

Telephone Number

E-mail Address

Gift

Save The Day Card Sent	Invitation Sent	R.S.V.P Received	Thank You Sent	Number Attending

Guest List Planner

Name

Address

Telephone Number

E-mail Address

Gift

| Save The Day Card Sent | Invitation Sent | R.S.V.P Received | Thank You Sent | Number Attending |

Name

Address

Telephone Number

E-mail Address

Gift

| Save The Day Card Sent | Invitation Sent | R.S.V.P Received | Thank You Sent | Number Attending |

Name

Address

Telephone Number

E-mail Address

Gift

| Save The Day Card Sent | Invitation Sent | R.S.V.P Received | Thank You Sent | Number Attending |

Name

Address

Telephone Number

E-mail Address

Gift

| Save The Day Card Sent | Invitation Sent | R.S.V.P Received | Thank You Sent | Number Attending |

Name

Address

Telephone Number

E-mail Address

Gift

| Save The Day Card Sent | Invitation Sent | R.S.V.P Received | Thank You Sent | Number Attending |

Guest List Planner

Name

Address

Telephone Number

E-mail Address

Gift

Save The Day Card Sent	Invitation Sent	R.S.V.P Received	Thank You Sent	Number Attending

Name

Address

Telephone Number

E-mail Address

Gift

Save The Day Card Sent	Invitation Sent	R.S.V.P Received	Thank You Sent	Number Attending

Name

Address

Telephone Number

E-mail Address

Gift

Save The Day Card Sent	Invitation Sent	R.S.V.P Received	Thank You Sent	Number Attending

Name

Address

Telephone Number

E-mail Address

Gift

Save The Day Card Sent	Invitation Sent	R.S.V.P Received	Thank You Sent	Number Attending

Name

Address

Telephone Number

E-mail Address

Gift

Save The Day Card Sent	Invitation Sent	R.S.V.P Received	Thank You Sent	Number Attending

Guest List Planner

Name

Address

Telephone Number

E-mail Address

Gift

| Save The Day Card Sent | Invitation Sent | R.S.V.P Received | Thank You Sent | Number Attending |

Name

Address

Telephone Number

E-mail Address

Gift

| Save The Day Card Sent | Invitation Sent | R.S.V.P Received | Thank You Sent | Number Attending |

Name

Address

Telephone Number

E-mail Address

Gift

| Save The Day Card Sent | Invitation Sent | R.S.V.P Received | Thank You Sent | Number Attending |

Name

Address

Telephone Number

E-mail Address

Gift

| Save The Day Card Sent | Invitation Sent | R.S.V.P Received | Thank You Sent | Number Attending |

Name

Address

Telephone Number

E-mail Address

Gift

| Save The Day Card Sent | Invitation Sent | R.S.V.P Received | Thank You Sent | Number Attending |

Guest List Planner

Name

Address

Telephone Number

E-mail Address

Gift

| Save The Day Card Sent | Invitation Sent | R.S.V.P Received | Thank You Sent | Number Attending |

Name

Address

Telephone Number

E-mail Address

Gift

| Save The Day Card Sent | Invitation Sent | R.S.V.P Received | Thank You Sent | Number Attending |

Name

Address

Telephone Number

E-mail Address

Gift

| Save The Day Card Sent | Invitation Sent | R.S.V.P Received | Thank You Sent | Number Attending |

Name

Address

Telephone Number

E-mail Address

Gift

| Save The Day Card Sent | Invitation Sent | R.S.V.P Received | Thank You Sent | Number Attending |

Name

Address

Telephone Number

E-mail Address

Gift

| Save The Day Card Sent | Invitation Sent | R.S.V.P Received | Thank You Sent | Number Attending |

Guest List Planner

Name

Address

Telephone Number

E-mail Address

Gift

| Save The Day Card Sent | Invitation Sent | R.S.V.P Received | Thank You Sent | Number Attending |

Name

Address

Telephone Number

E-mail Address

Gift

| Save The Day Card Sent | Invitation Sent | R.S.V.P Received | Thank You Sent | Number Attending |

Name

Address

Telephone Number

E-mail Address

Gift

| Save The Day Card Sent | Invitation Sent | R.S.V.P Received | Thank You Sent | Number Attending |

Name

Address

Telephone Number

E-mail Address

Gift

| Save The Day Card Sent | Invitation Sent | R.S.V.P Received | Thank You Sent | Number Attending |

Name

Address

Telephone Number

E-mail Address

Gift

| Save The Day Card Sent | Invitation Sent | R.S.V.P Received | Thank You Sent | Number Attending |

Guest List Planner

Name

Address

Telephone Number

E-mail Address

Gift

Save The Day Card Sent	Invitation Sent	R.S.V.P Received	Thank You Sent	Number Attending

Name

Address

Telephone Number

E-mail Address

Gift

Save The Day Card Sent	Invitation Sent	R.S.V.P Received	Thank You Sent	Number Attending

Name

Address

Telephone Number

E-mail Address

Gift

Save The Day Card Sent	Invitation Sent	R.S.V.P Received	Thank You Sent	Number Attending

Name

Address

Telephone Number

E-mail Address

Gift

Save The Day Card Sent	Invitation Sent	R.S.V.P Received	Thank You Sent	Number Attending

Name

Address

Telephone Number

E-mail Address

Gift

Save The Day Card Sent	Invitation Sent	R.S.V.P Received	Thank You Sent	Number Attending

Guest List Planner

Name

Address

Telephone Number

E-mail Address

Gift

Save The Day Card Sent	Invitation Sent	R.S.V.P Received	Thank You Sent	Number Attending

Name

Address

Telephone Number

E-mail Address

Gift

Save The Day Card Sent	Invitation Sent	R.S.V.P Received	Thank You Sent	Number Attending

Name

Address

Telephone Number

E-mail Address

Gift

Save The Day Card Sent	Invitation Sent	R.S.V.P Received	Thank You Sent	Number Attending

Name

Address

Telephone Number

E-mail Address

Gift

Save The Day Card Sent	Invitation Sent	R.S.V.P Received	Thank You Sent	Number Attending

Name

Address

Telephone Number

E-mail Address

Gift

Save The Day Card Sent	Invitation Sent	R.S.V.P Received	Thank You Sent	Number Attending

Guest List Planner

Name

Address

Telephone Number

E-mail Address

Gift

Save The Day Card Sent	Invitation Sent	R.S.V.P Received	Thank You Sent	Number Attending

Name

Address

Telephone Number

E-mail Address

Gift

Save The Day Card Sent	Invitation Sent	R.S.V.P Received	Thank You Sent	Number Attending

Name

Address

Telephone Number

E-mail Address

Gift

Save The Day Card Sent	Invitation Sent	R.S.V.P Received	Thank You Sent	Number Attending

Name

Address

Telephone Number

E-mail Address

Gift

Save The Day Card Sent	Invitation Sent	R.S.V.P Received	Thank You Sent	Number Attending

Name

Address

Telephone Number

E-mail Address

Gift

Save The Day Card Sent	Invitation Sent	R.S.V.P Received	Thank You Sent	Number Attending

Guest List Planner

Name _____
Address _____
Telephone Number _____
E-mail Address _____
Gift _____

Save The Day Card Sent	Invitation Sent	R.S.V.P Received	Thank You Sent	Number Attending
_____	_____	_____	_____	_____

Name _____
Address _____
Telephone Number _____
E-mail Address _____
Gift _____

Save The Day Card Sent	Invitation Sent	R.S.V.P Received	Thank You Sent	Number Attending
_____	_____	_____	_____	_____

Name _____
Address _____
Telephone Number _____
E-mail Address _____
Gift _____

Save The Day Card Sent	Invitation Sent	R.S.V.P Received	Thank You Sent	Number Attending
_____	_____	_____	_____	_____

Name _____
Address _____
Telephone Number _____
E-mail Address _____
Gift _____

Save The Day Card Sent	Invitation Sent	R.S.V.P Received	Thank You Sent	Number Attending
_____	_____	_____	_____	_____

Name _____
Address _____
Telephone Number _____
E-mail Address _____
Gift _____

Save The Day Card Sent	Invitation Sent	R.S.V.P Received	Thank You Sent	Number Attending
_____	_____	_____	_____	_____

Guest List Planner

Name

Address

Telephone Number

E-mail Address

Gift

Save The Day Card Sent	Invitation Sent	R.S.V.P Received	Thank You Sent	Number Attending

Name

Address

Telephone Number

E-mail Address

Gift

Save The Day Card Sent	Invitation Sent	R.S.V.P Received	Thank You Sent	Number Attending

Name

Address

Telephone Number

E-mail Address

Gift

Save The Day Card Sent	Invitation Sent	R.S.V.P Received	Thank You Sent	Number Attending

Name

Address

Telephone Number

E-mail Address

Gift

Save The Day Card Sent	Invitation Sent	R.S.V.P Received	Thank You Sent	Number Attending

Name

Address

Telephone Number

E-mail Address

Gift

Save The Day Card Sent	Invitation Sent	R.S.V.P Received	Thank You Sent	Number Attending

Guest List Planner

Name

Address

Telephone Number

E-mail Address

Gift

| Save The Day Card Sent | Invitation Sent | R.S.V.P Received | Thank You Sent | Number Attending |

Name

Address

Telephone Number

E-mail Address

Gift

| Save The Day Card Sent | Invitation Sent | R.S.V.P Received | Thank You Sent | Number Attending |

Name

Address

Telephone Number

E-mail Address

Gift

| Save The Day Card Sent | Invitation Sent | R.S.V.P Received | Thank You Sent | Number Attending |

Name

Address

Telephone Number

E-mail Address

Gift

| Save The Day Card Sent | Invitation Sent | R.S.V.P Received | Thank You Sent | Number Attending |

Name

Address

Telephone Number

E-mail Address

Gift

| Save The Day Card Sent | Invitation Sent | R.S.V.P Received | Thank You Sent | Number Attending |

Guest List Planner

Name

Address

Telephone Number

E-mail Address

Gift

| Save The Day Card Sent | Invitation Sent | R.S.V.P Received | Thank You Sent | Number Attending |

Name

Address

Telephone Number

E-mail Address

Gift

| Save The Day Card Sent | Invitation Sent | R.S.V.P Received | Thank You Sent | Number Attending |

Name

Address

Telephone Number

E-mail Address

Gift

| Save The Day Card Sent | Invitation Sent | R.S.V.P Received | Thank You Sent | Number Attending |

Name

Address

Telephone Number

E-mail Address

Gift

| Save The Day Card Sent | Invitation Sent | R.S.V.P Received | Thank You Sent | Number Attending |

Name

Address

Telephone Number

E-mail Address

Gift

| Save The Day Card Sent | Invitation Sent | R.S.V.P Received | Thank You Sent | Number Attending |

Guest List Planner

Name

Address

Telephone Number

E-mail Address

Gift

Save The Day Card Sent	Invitation Sent	R.S.V.P Received	Thank You Sent	Number Attending

Name

Address

Telephone Number

E-mail Address

Gift

Save The Day Card Sent	Invitation Sent	R.S.V.P Received	Thank You Sent	Number Attending

Name

Address

Telephone Number

E-mail Address

Gift

Save The Day Card Sent	Invitation Sent	R.S.V.P Received	Thank You Sent	Number Attending

Name

Address

Telephone Number

E-mail Address

Gift

Save The Day Card Sent	Invitation Sent	R.S.V.P Received	Thank You Sent	Number Attending

Name

Address

Telephone Number

E-mail Address

Gift

Save The Day Card Sent	Invitation Sent	R.S.V.P Received	Thank You Sent	Number Attending

Guest List Planner

Name

Address

Telephone Number

E-mail Address

Gift

Save The Day Card Sent	Invitation Sent	R.S.V.P Received	Thank You Sent	Number Attending

Name

Address

Telephone Number

E-mail Address

Gift

Save The Day Card Sent	Invitation Sent	R.S.V.P Received	Thank You Sent	Number Attending

Name

Address

Telephone Number

E-mail Address

Gift

Save The Day Card Sent	Invitation Sent	R.S.V.P Received	Thank You Sent	Number Attending

Name

Address

Telephone Number

E-mail Address

Gift

Save The Day Card Sent	Invitation Sent	R.S.V.P Received	Thank You Sent	Number Attending

Name

Address

Telephone Number

E-mail Address

Gift

Save The Day Card Sent	Invitation Sent	R.S.V.P Received	Thank You Sent	Number Attending

Guest List Planner

Name

Address

Telephone Number

E-mail Address

Gift

Save The Day Card Sent	Invitation Sent	R.S.V.P Received	Thank You Sent	Number Attending

Name

Address

Telephone Number

E-mail Address

Gift

Save The Day Card Sent	Invitation Sent	R.S.V.P Received	Thank You Sent	Number Attending

Name

Address

Telephone Number

E-mail Address

Gift

Save The Day Card Sent	Invitation Sent	R.S.V.P Received	Thank You Sent	Number Attending

Name

Address

Telephone Number

E-mail Address

Gift

Save The Day Card Sent	Invitation Sent	R.S.V.P Received	Thank You Sent	Number Attending

Name

Address

Telephone Number

E-mail Address

Gift

Save The Day Card Sent	Invitation Sent	R.S.V.P Received	Thank You Sent	Number Attending

Guest List Planner

Name

Address

Telephone Number

E-mail Address

Gift

Save The Day Card Sent	Invitation Sent	R.S.V.P Received	Thank You Sent	Number Attending

Name

Address

Telephone Number

E-mail Address

Gift

Save The Day Card Sent	Invitation Sent	R.S.V.P Received	Thank You Sent	Number Attending

Name

Address

Telephone Number

E-mail Address

Gift

Save The Day Card Sent	Invitation Sent	R.S.V.P Received	Thank You Sent	Number Attending

Name

Address

Telephone Number

E-mail Address

Gift

Save The Day Card Sent	Invitation Sent	R.S.V.P Received	Thank You Sent	Number Attending

Name

Address

Telephone Number

E-mail Address

Gift

Save The Day Card Sent	Invitation Sent	R.S.V.P Received	Thank You Sent	Number Attending

Guest List Planner

Name

Address

Telephone Number

E-mail Address

Gift

Save The Day Card Sent	Invitation Sent	R.S.V.P Received	Thank You Sent	Number Attending

Name

Address

Telephone Number

E-mail Address

Gift

Save The Day Card Sent	Invitation Sent	R.S.V.P Received	Thank You Sent	Number Attending

Name

Address

Telephone Number

E-mail Address

Gift

Save The Day Card Sent	Invitation Sent	R.S.V.P Received	Thank You Sent	Number Attending

Name

Address

Telephone Number

E-mail Address

Gift

Save The Day Card Sent	Invitation Sent	R.S.V.P Received	Thank You Sent	Number Attending

Name

Address

Telephone Number

E-mail Address

Gift

Save The Day Card Sent	Invitation Sent	R.S.V.P Received	Thank You Sent	Number Attending

Guest List Planner

Name

Address

Telephone Number

E-mail Address

Gift

Save The Day Card Sent	Invitation Sent	R.S.V.P Received	Thank You Sent	Number Attending

Name

Address

Telephone Number

E-mail Address

Gift

Save The Day Card Sent	Invitation Sent	R.S.V.P Received	Thank You Sent	Number Attending

Name

Address

Telephone Number

E-mail Address

Gift

Save The Day Card Sent	Invitation Sent	R.S.V.P Received	Thank You Sent	Number Attending

Name

Address

Telephone Number

E-mail Address

Gift

Save The Day Card Sent	Invitation Sent	R.S.V.P Received	Thank You Sent	Number Attending

Name

Address

Telephone Number

E-mail Address

Gift

Save The Day Card Sent	Invitation Sent	R.S.V.P Received	Thank You Sent	Number Attending

Guest List Planner

Name

Address

Telephone Number

E-mail Address

Gift

| Save The Day Card Sent | Invitation Sent | R.S.V.P Received | Thank You Sent | Number Attending |

Name

Address

Telephone Number

E-mail Address

Gift

| Save The Day Card Sent | Invitation Sent | R.S.V.P Received | Thank You Sent | Number Attending |

Name

Address

Telephone Number

E-mail Address

Gift

| Save The Day Card Sent | Invitation Sent | R.S.V.P Received | Thank You Sent | Number Attending |

Name

Address

Telephone Number

E-mail Address

Gift

| Save The Day Card Sent | Invitation Sent | R.S.V.P Received | Thank You Sent | Number Attending |

Name

Address

Telephone Number

E-mail Address

Gift

| Save The Day Card Sent | Invitation Sent | R.S.V.P Received | Thank You Sent | Number Attending |

Guest List Planner

Name

Address

Telephone Number

E-mail Address

Gift

Save The Day Card Sent	Invitation Sent	R.S.V.P Received	Thank You Sent	Number Attending

Name

Address

Telephone Number

E-mail Address

Gift

Save The Day Card Sent	Invitation Sent	R.S.V.P Received	Thank You Sent	Number Attending

Name

Address

Telephone Number

E-mail Address

Gift

Save The Day Card Sent	Invitation Sent	R.S.V.P Received	Thank You Sent	Number Attending

Name

Address

Telephone Number

E-mail Address

Gift

Save The Day Card Sent	Invitation Sent	R.S.V.P Received	Thank You Sent	Number Attending

Name

Address

Telephone Number

E-mail Address

Gift

Save The Day Card Sent	Invitation Sent	R.S.V.P Received	Thank You Sent	Number Attending

Guest List Planner

Name

Address

Telephone Number

E-mail Address

Gift

Save The Day Card Sent	Invitation Sent	R.S.V.P Received	Thank You Sent	Number Attending

Name

Address

Telephone Number

E-mail Address

Gift

Save The Day Card Sent	Invitation Sent	R.S.V.P Received	Thank You Sent	Number Attending

Name

Address

Telephone Number

E-mail Address

Gift

Save The Day Card Sent	Invitation Sent	R.S.V.P Received	Thank You Sent	Number Attending

Name

Address

Telephone Number

E-mail Address

Gift

Save The Day Card Sent	Invitation Sent	R.S.V.P Received	Thank You Sent	Number Attending

Name

Address

Telephone Number

E-mail Address

Gift

Save The Day Card Sent	Invitation Sent	R.S.V.P Received	Thank You Sent	Number Attending

Guest List Planner

Name

Address

Telephone Number

E-mail Address

Gift

Save The Day Card Sent	Invitation Sent	R.S.V.P Received	Thank You Sent	Number Attending

Name

Address

Telephone Number

E-mail Address

Gift

Save The Day Card Sent	Invitation Sent	R.S.V.P Received	Thank You Sent	Number Attending

Name

Address

Telephone Number

E-mail Address

Gift

Save The Day Card Sent	Invitation Sent	R.S.V.P Received	Thank You Sent	Number Attending

Name

Address

Telephone Number

E-mail Address

Gift

Save The Day Card Sent	Invitation Sent	R.S.V.P Received	Thank You Sent	Number Attending

Name

Address

Telephone Number

E-mail Address

Gift

Save The Day Card Sent	Invitation Sent	R.S.V.P Received	Thank You Sent	Number Attending

Guest List Planner

Name

Address

Telephone Number

E-mail Address

Gift

Save The Day Card Sent	Invitation Sent	R.S.V.P Received	Thank You Sent	Number Attending

Name

Address

Telephone Number

E-mail Address

Gift

Save The Day Card Sent	Invitation Sent	R.S.V.P Received	Thank You Sent	Number Attending

Name

Address

Telephone Number

E-mail Address

Gift

Save The Day Card Sent	Invitation Sent	R.S.V.P Received	Thank You Sent	Number Attending

Name

Address

Telephone Number

E-mail Address

Gift

Save The Day Card Sent	Invitation Sent	R.S.V.P Received	Thank You Sent	Number Attending

Name

Address

Telephone Number

E-mail Address

Gift

Save The Day Card Sent	Invitation Sent	R.S.V.P Received	Thank You Sent	Number Attending

Guest List Planner

Name

Address

Telephone Number

E-mail Address

Gift

Save The Day Card Sent	Invitation Sent	R.S.V.P Received	Thank You Sent	Number Attending

Name

Address

Telephone Number

E-mail Address

Gift

Save The Day Card Sent	Invitation Sent	R.S.V.P Received	Thank You Sent	Number Attending

Name

Address

Telephone Number

E-mail Address

Gift

Save The Day Card Sent	Invitation Sent	R.S.V.P Received	Thank You Sent	Number Attending

Name

Address

Telephone Number

E-mail Address

Gift

Save The Day Card Sent	Invitation Sent	R.S.V.P Received	Thank You Sent	Number Attending

Name

Address

Telephone Number

E-mail Address

Gift

Save The Day Card Sent	Invitation Sent	R.S.V.P Received	Thank You Sent	Number Attending

Guest List Planner

Name

Address

Telephone Number

E-mail Address

Gift

Save The Day Card Sent	Invitation Sent	R.S.V.P Received	Thank You Sent	Number Attending

Name

Address

Telephone Number

E-mail Address

Gift

Save The Day Card Sent	Invitation Sent	R.S.V.P Received	Thank You Sent	Number Attending

Name

Address

Telephone Number

E-mail Address

Gift

Save The Day Card Sent	Invitation Sent	R.S.V.P Received	Thank You Sent	Number Attending

Name

Address

Telephone Number

E-mail Address

Gift

Save The Day Card Sent	Invitation Sent	R.S.V.P Received	Thank You Sent	Number Attending

Name

Address

Telephone Number

E-mail Address

Gift

Save The Day Card Sent	Invitation Sent	R.S.V.P Received	Thank You Sent	Number Attending

Guest List Planner

Name

Address

Telephone Number

E-mail Address

Gift

| Save The Day Card Sent | Invitation Sent | R.S.V.P Received | Thank You Sent | Number Attending |

Name

Address

Telephone Number

E-mail Address

Gift

| Save The Day Card Sent | Invitation Sent | R.S.V.P Received | Thank You Sent | Number Attending |

Name

Address

Telephone Number

E-mail Address

Gift

| Save The Day Card Sent | Invitation Sent | R.S.V.P Received | Thank You Sent | Number Attending |

Name

Address

Telephone Number

E-mail Address

Gift

| Save The Day Card Sent | Invitation Sent | R.S.V.P Received | Thank You Sent | Number Attending |

Name

Address

Telephone Number

E-mail Address

Gift

| Save The Day Card Sent | Invitation Sent | R.S.V.P Received | Thank You Sent | Number Attending |

Printed by Amazon Italia Logistica S.r.l.
Torrazza Piemonte (TO), Italy